GAMBIA, GHANA, LIBERIA, AND SIERRA LEONE

GAMBIA, GHANA, LIBERIA, AND SIERRA LEONE.

BY HENRY GILFOND

FRANKLIN WATTS
New York | London | Toronto | Sydney | 1981
A FIRST BOOK

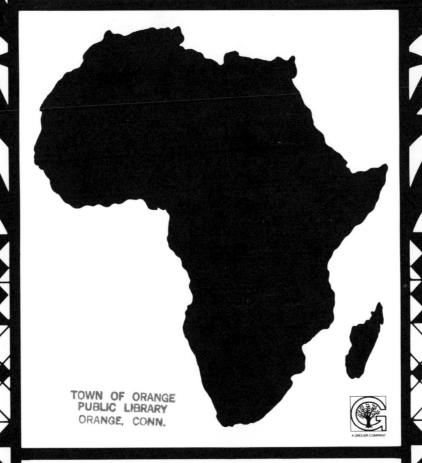

A GROLIER COMPANY

Cover design by Jackie Schuman

Photographs courtesy of:
Allen Rokach: pp. 10, 17, 24, 29;
Sygma/UNICEF photo by Hewett: p. 36;
United Nations/B. Wolff: pp. 47, 56;
World Bank Photo by Pamela Johnson: p. 50.

Maps courtesy of Vantage Art, Inc.

Library of Congress Cataloging in Publication Data

Gilfond, Henry.
Gambia, Ghana, Liberia, and Sierra Leone.
(A First book)
Bibliography: p.
Includes index.
SUMMARY: Covers the land, wildlife, people,
languages, family, religion, education, health,
resources, and history of four countries
located in the bulge of West Africa.
1. Africa, West—Juvenile literature.
[1. Africa, West] I. Title.
DT471.G545   966   80-23043
ISBN 0-531-04274-X

To Jean and Milton

CONTENTS

GAMBIA, GHANA, LIBERIA, AND SIERRA LEONE

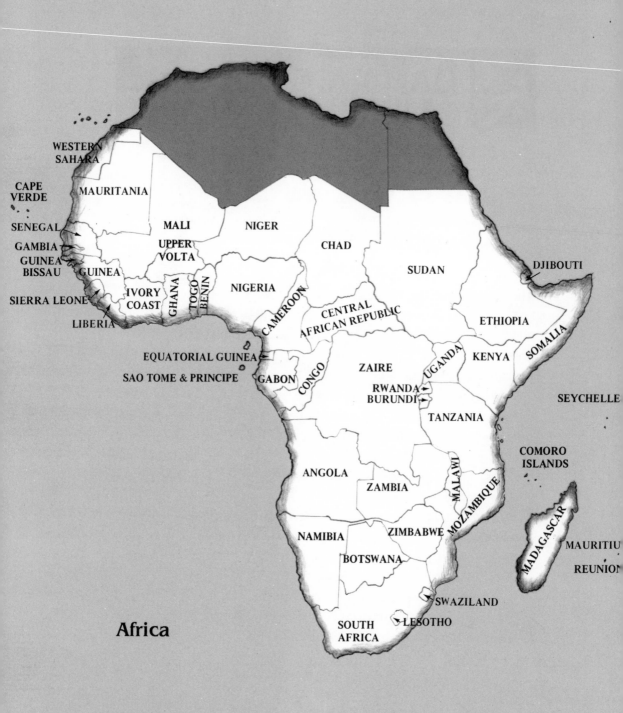

WESTERN
SAHARA

CAPE
VERDE

MAURITANIA

SENEGAL

GAMBIA

GUINEA
BISSAU

GUINEA

SIERRA LEONE

LIBERIA

IVORY
COAST

MALI

UPPER
VOLTA

GHANA

TOGO

BENIN

NIGER

NIGERIA

CAMEROON

CHAD

SUDAN

DJIBOUTI

CENTRAL
AFRICAN REPUBLIC

ETHIOPIA

SOMALIA

EQUATORIAL GUINEA

SAO TOME & PRINCIPE

GABON

CONGO

ZAIRE

UGANDA

RWANDA

BURUNDI

KENYA

SEYCHELLE

TANZANIA

COMORO
ISLANDS

ANGOLA

ZAMBIA

MALAWI

MOZAMBIQUE

MADAGASCAR

MAURITIU

REUNION

NAMIBIA

ZIMBABWE

BOTSWANA

SWAZILAND

LESOTHO

SOUTH
AFRICA

Africa

1
GAMBIA, GHANA, LIBERIA, AND SIERRA LEONE

The Portuguese, in 1482, ten years before Christopher Columbus sailed to America, established the first European trading posts in the great bulge of West Africa. Their first post was set up in what is now called Ghana. They were also the first Europeans to set up posts in Gambia and Sierra Leone.

All the territory of the West African bulge, which at the time included Liberia, Gambia, Ghana, and Sierra Leone, was broken up into a number of different independent kingdoms and chiefdoms. The Portuguese wanted the gold that seemed plentiful in the area and had no trouble trading mostly firearms for the precious metal.

The Dutch, Danes, French, Germans, and British followed the Portuguese lead, establishing their own posts in Africa, and forts to protect them. The British established settlements of their own people in this part of Africa, too.

The rivalry among these Europeans for the spoils of Africa, especially when slave trading became more profitable than gold trading, led to open warfare. Beginning early in the seventeenth century, slaves were in great demand in the West Indies and America, and the number of slaves that could be wrenched from Africa was enormous.

Great Britain, with the most powerful navy in the world, had become "Mistress of the Seas" after defeating the Spanish Armada in 1588, and was able to oust the Portuguese from Gambia. They bought land from the different chiefs of the Gambian peoples and withstood the efforts of the Danes, Swedes, French, and Germans to take over the territory. Gambia became Britain's first African colony.

Ghana, at the time called the Gold Coast, became a British colony, too. The Dutch had driven out the first settlers in the Gold Coast, the Portuguese. The Dutch, in turn, were ousted by the British, who held on to the land for about two hundred years, until 1957.

The British encountered little resistance in occupying the coastal area of Ghana. They had considerable difficulty, however, pushing inland, where the Ashanti people would not be governed by the British. The Ashanti fought long and hard before they submitted to the greatly superior force of the British.

Britain extended and deepened its control in West Africa after Parliament outlawed slave trading in 1807. With the profit taken out of the slave trade, the Dutch, Portuguese, Danes, and the other Europeans quit Africa, leaving the British a free hand to develop their interest in the territories as they saw fit.

There is no accurate count today of the number of West African men, women, and children who were sold into slavery. By the year 1600 some nine hundred thousand were torn from their African homes and shipped to the British West Indies. At least three million more were carried in slave ships to Britain's American colonies in the seventeenth century. The slave ships carried another eleven million slaves to America in the eighteenth and nineteenth centuries. These are considered to be low estimates and do not account for the great number of slaves who died on the slave ships.

The numbers are even more appalling when we consider the size of these countries. Together, the area of these countries is just a bit larger than the state of California.

Sad to say, a number of African chiefs promoted this inhuman traffic in slavery. A certain number of criminals, though not very many, were sold to the slave traders. A far greater number of men, women, and children sold into slavery were prisoners of the wars between the different chiefs and kings of the territory. At times, it is believed, a number of chiefs went on raiding parties, if not to war, for the sole purpose of capturing prisoners for the slave trade, and profiting from it.

There was, however, considerable and often violent opposition to this slave traffic among the African peoples themselves. The enslaved people sought every avenue of escape, and often did escape. There were armed rebellions both in Africa and on the slave ships.

The colony of Sierra Leone was created in 1788 as a haven for freed slaves from Britain, and for the runaway slaves from America, and for those who had escaped the slave traders in Africa.

Liberia was created in 1822 by Americans for a similar purpose, but was limited to slaves who had been freed in America. Liberia, incidentally, was established as a free and independent country. In fact, it was the first black republic on the continent of Africa.

THE LAND

All four of the countries in the West African bulge border on the South Atlantic Ocean. Except for Gambia, which is a very tiny country, they all have extended coastlines. They all have excellent harbors—Banjul in Gambia, Takoradi in Ghana, Freetown in Sierra Leone, and Monrovia in Liberia. Freetown is the third largest harbor in the world. Sir John Hawkins and Sir Francis Drake, two of England's most celebrated sea captains and pirates, left their names in the history of that harbor. Sir John ravaged the area in 1564. Sir Francis left his name on a stone there in 1579. During World War II three hundred ships, including the *Queen Mary* and the *Queen Elizabeth,* found protective anchorage in the Freetown harbor.

The bulge of West Africa is all in an area known as the Torrid Zone, north of the equator and south of the Tropic of Cancer. Like all lands in the Torrid Zone, the bulge has two seasons in the year, the rainy season and the dry season. Its land, then, is much like any other in the tropics.

The shorelines have long stretches of sandy beaches, mangrove swamps and lagoons, sand dunes, and sometimes sandy cliffs. Further inland there are grass strips, then hilly woodlands, rolling hills, plateaus, and sometimes mountains. There are rain forests, too, and Liberia has a huge area of rubber trees. Near the northeastern frontier of Liberia, Mount Nimba and surrounding mountains climb to a height of 4,200 feet (1,280 m). Toward the northwest, the Wale Mountains rise to a height of 4,500 feet (1,370 m). In Sierra Leone an arid plateau ranges in height from 1,000 to 2,000 feet (305 to 610 m) with some peaks that are more than 6,000 feet (1,830 m) high.

The rivers in these lands are plentiful, and navigable. The

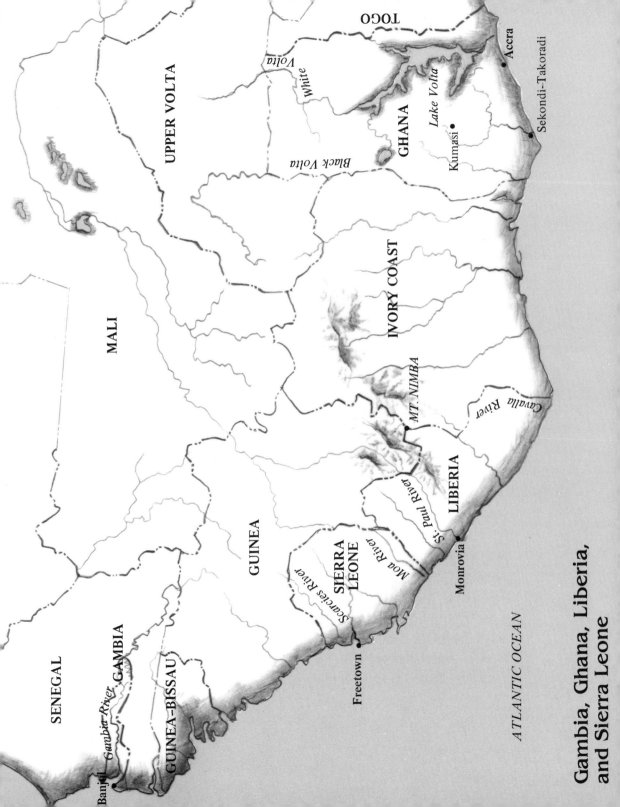

Gambia, Ghana, Liberia,
and Sierra Leone

SENEGAL

MALI

UPPER VOLTA

GUINEA-BISSAU

GUINEA

Gambia River

GAMBIA

Banjul

SIERRA
LEONE

Scarcies River

Moa River

Freetown

St. Paul River

LIBERIA

Monrovia

IVORY COAST

MT. NIMBA

Cavalla River

Black Volta

White

Volta

GHANA

Lake Volta

Kumasi

TOGO

Accra

Sekondi-Takoradi

ATLANTIC OCEAN

Gambia River runs through the entire length of Gambia, about 300 miles (480 km). Among the more important rivers of Ghana are the Volta, the Pra, and the Ankobra. Liberia has the Saint Paul River and the Cavalla River. Sierra Leone has five important rivers, the Sewa, the Moa, the Jong, the Rokel, and the Scarcies.

VEGETATION

Trees grow abundantly in the tropical bulge. Palm trees, acacia trees, cottonwoods, and baobabs are numerous. So are cacao trees, particularly in Ghana. There is much scrub brush in this area, and there are coffee trees, too, mostly in Ghana and Liberia.

Rice grows in all four of these countries of the West African bulge. So does cassava, a plant with a starchy root. There is a good deal of sugarcane in Liberia and considerable cotton in Ghana.

Fruits and vegetables, as might be expected in the climate of these tropical countries, are plentiful as are a variety of nuts, and palm kernels. Peanuts are in such abundance that 95 percent of Gambia's exports are peanuts, known in Africa as groundnuts.

WILDLIFE

Hunting has eliminated much of the wildlife in the West African bulge, but it is far from gone. Antelope, monkeys, manatees, pygmy hippopotamuses, dwarf buffalo, and leopards thrive in the tropical climate. So do baboons, chimpanzees, civet cats, hyenas, among many other animals that live in the hills, plateaus, and woodlands of these countries.

There are cobras, puff adders, vipers, and mambas, all dangerous snakes. There is a host of other snakes that are quite harmless, as well as lizards, turtles, and tortoises.

There are crocodiles, too. Some are quite peaceful. At Berending, in Gambia, women wash their clothes and children swim in a river infested with crocodiles, known as the Sacred Crocodiles of Berending.

Birds in the tropics are most often very beautiful but sometimes strange in appearance. There are herons, egrets, cardinals, kingfishers, jays, and flamingoes. There are storks, pelicans, the grotesque hornbill touracos, and weaverbirds. Among the vultures, there is the hawk, the owl, and the fish eagle.

Fish, too, are plentiful off the coast of West Africa. There are butterfish, herring, ladyfish, snappers, sheepsheads, shine-noses, and mackerel. There are also tuna and barracuda. Inland, in many of the rivers, there are trout. There are also many shell-fish: shrimp, oysters, and rock lobsters.

It should be noted that there has been considerable effort by the different countries of this area to control the hunting of wildlife. To date, however, they have not been very successful with such programs.

2
PEOPLES AND LANGUAGES

Gambia, Ghana, Liberia, and Sierra Leone have shared a rather common history. They have also shared a relatively common culture. At one time or another they were all part of, or greatly influenced by, the great ancient African empires of Ghana, Mali, and Songhai. (The countries of Ghana and Mali are not to be confused with those empires. Present-day Ghana and Mali assumed their names when they became independent countries, to honor the richest and most powerful empires in the history of Africa.)

After the decline and disintegration of these empires in the fifteenth century, the countries of West Africa, again in common, suffered at the hands of invaders. The invaders were Berbers who came from North Africa and the Sahara region, as well as on the ships of the seafaring countries of Europe: France, Holland, Denmark, Sweden, Portugal, and England. Three of them became British colonies: Gambia, Ghana, and Sierra Leone. Liberia was more or less a protectorate of the United States.

Still, for all the sameness in their past histories, there are major differences among them. There are differences in their natural resources, their agriculture, and their industries. They are all republics, but the forms of those republics are different. There are also differences in their recent histories and differences in the nature of their populations as well.

A great number of different ethnic groups inhabit these countries. There are people of many different clans, tribes, small chiefdoms, and small kingdoms. As a matter of fact, each of these four countries is the home of a conglomeration of different peoples who migrated to them from many different parts of Africa. Liberia and Sierra Leone, in addition, have a population of the descendants of freed British and American slaves. And each of these peoples brought its own language, tradition, and religion to its new home.

In tiny Gambia there are the Mandingo people, the Fula, Wolof, Serahili, and Jola, among others.

In Ghana there are the Guan people, the Akan, and the warlike Ashanti who once ruled an empire and who maintained their own kingdom into the twentieth century. Among the many other peoples of Ghana are the Twi, Ewe, Gonja, Kassena, Nankani, Builsa, Wala, Fanti, and Ga-Adangbe. The Fanti and the Ga-Adangbe carried on an international trade for more than four centuries.

Liberia has a relatively small population of Creoles, descendants of freed American slaves, and no one knows from what part of Africa their ancestors came. Among the greater number of different peoples in Liberia are the Cai, Mende, Kpelle, Bassa, Dey, and Gribo. The Gribo people are skilled sailors. They also take great pride in saying that they have always been free, never slaves.

Thirty percent of the people of Sierra Leone are Mende people who live mostly in the northern areas of the country. Another 30 percent of the many peoples of Sierra Leone, living mostly in the south, are the Temne people. Others are the Yalunk, Koranko, Kono, Krim, Kissi, Gola, Kru, Fula, Lokko, and Limba. The Limba people are probably the oldest inhabitants of Sierra Leone.

Each of these countries in the West African bulge is obviously something of a melting pot of almost countless different African peoples. The one trait in common to all of them is a fierce love for freedom and independence, the same love found in other peoples all over the world. But the presence of so many different ethnic groups in the relatively small areas of Ghana, Gambia, Liberia, and Sierra Leone has made for any number of difficulties. National unity, the creating of one united people out of this conglomeration of so many varied clans, tribes, and kingdoms, has been one of the most delicate and difficult problems of these young African nations.

LANGUAGES

English is the official language in Gambia, Ghana, Liberia, and Sierra Leone, since three of them were British colonies. Liberia was an Afro-American republic. But, in each of these coun-

A craftsman in Ghana works beneath the words of Marcus Garvey and H. Rap Brown, two important men in the movement for black freedom.

tries, English is spoken by only a minority of the population. In West Africa, as already indicated, there are as many different languages spoken as there are ethnic groups.

Mandinka and Wolof, African tribal languages, are spoken by the majority of people in Gambia. In Ghana the people speak about fifty different languages and dialects, including Twi, Fanti, Ga, Ewe, Hausa, Dagbani, Nizima, and Akan. Akan, itself, is spoken in some sixty-five different dialects.

The Liberians speak about twenty-eight different languages native to Africa, and many dialects as well.

In Sierra Leone, the different peoples speak a host of African tongues. In addition, there is pidgin English, which is spoken by the freed slaves who settled in the country. Pidgin English is generally called Creole in Sierra Leone and is a language that is a mixture of English, Portuguese and other European languages, elements of fourteen West African languages, and various dialects brought with the freed slaves from the British West Indies.

It is estimated that there are more than eight hundred languages spoken in Africa that are native to the continent. And all these languages are highly developed. They are expressive and allow for developing vocabularies.

Actually, there are families of languages in Africa. All the different languages of Gambia, Ghana, Liberia, and Sierra Leone belong to one such family, the Niger-Congo family. But this does not mean that a clan speaking Susu will understand a clan speaking Mandingo. There is a special quality common to all African tongues. African languages are tonal in quality. That is, the meaning of words often depends on the pitch or tone with which a word, or even just a syllable, is spoken.

It is interesting to note that the tonal quality of African speech can be almost perfectly duplicated by certain kinds of African drums. The Africans call them "talking drums," and they are used for sending and receiving messages over long distances all over the African continent.

3

THE FAMILY IN THE WEST AFRICAN BULGE

West Africans, like all Africans, are strongly loyal to their clans and communities. They are most loyal, however, to their families. This is particularly true in the small villages and other rural areas, where Europeans and Americans have had little effect on the ways of their lives.

More and more people are moving into the larger towns and cities, for work opportunities and for better educational possibilities. The great majority of the people, however, stay in the rural districts, where they were born and feel more comfortable with their customs and the faith and traditions of their ancestors.

They live in the rain forest area, just beyond the coastline; or in the plateaus further inland, herding their small flocks of sheep and goats and cattle. The city dwellers house their families in modern homes, if they are affluent. But more often, the city people live in shacks. In the rural areas, homes usually consist of mud-brick walls and a thatched roof. Wealthier rural people will have corrugated iron for their roofs.

The men of the family will find jobs in the mines, in lumber camps, or on some of the richer plantations. The women, for the most part, work in the community and at home. In addition to the household chores of cooking, sewing, weaving, cleaning, and mending, women do the weeding in the fields of their own small holding or in the cooperative farms. They also do the transplanting of crops and join in the harvesting, threshing the grain, winnowing, and milling.

Curiously, it is the women in the family who most frequently carry the family crops and handiwork to the markets. They are the sellers and traders. In Ghana, there are so many women merchants and traders that they have organized the Federation of Market Associations in Accra, the capital city of Ghana.

Women, by tradition, have always been highly respected in Africa. In ancient times women went about wearing bracelets and collars that otherwise were worn only by their kings. They also held some of the more important posts in their kingdoms and had a great deal of power. There were women who controlled whole villages. Muslim travelers were amazed by the personal liberty and the social positions of the African women. They are still amazed.

Today the women of Gambia, Ghana, Liberia, and Sierra Leone hold religious and politically responsible posts. Annie Jiagge, for example, is a judge in Ghana's highly prestigious court of appeals. Kate Abbam is the editor-in-chief of *Obaa Sima* ("Ideal Woman"), an influential magazine in Accra, Ghana's capital.

Before the recent military coup, women in Liberia held such important posts as assistant secretary for public works, commissioner of writs, and assistant district attorney. Mrs.

Ella Koblo Gulama is an elected member of Sierra Leone's House of Representatives.

These women are the exceptional women in West Africa, and though they are growing in number, women for the most part do not have the social status of the men in their communities. Like most women all over the world, their primary responsibilities are the home and the children.

Children are considered the most important members of the family. They are the ones who will carry on the family line, and its traditions. The present may be for the older people. The future is definitely for the children.

From early on, children are taught the manners, the laws and the customs of their people. They are taught to respect their elders and, if the family is Muslim, to be good Muslims. If the faith of the family is one of the many other faiths of the African peoples, they are taught to respect their ancestors as well. Almost all religions indigenous to Africa hold that there are obligations demanded of them by their ancestors. If they fail to carry out these obligations, the ancestors will cause them to suffer some illness or other misfortune.

Life can be very difficult in the rural areas, and parents teach their children the rudiments of survival. Children learn early about the nature of the land they live in, what makes

Appointed by the people in her village of Mepe, Ghana, this woman is in charge of all the problems concerning the women in the town.

[16]

good crops and how to grow things to eat. They are taught which shrubs, grasses, and berries they can eat, and which they cannot. They are also taught which animals, snakes, and insects are dangerous, and which are harmless.

The formal schooling of children in reading, writing, and arithmetic, particularly those in the rural areas, has only recently become a concern for parents. The governments of Gambia, Ghana, Liberia, and Sierra Leone have spent a great amount of money, and energy, to bring this sort of education to their young people, and the older people have welcomed the government programs. It has been difficult, however, for the poor families of the rural areas to keep their children in school, when they are still needed to help till the land.

Almost all the food for the family, especially rural families, comes from their own land. Rice is their staple. Their grain is usually sorghum or millet, grain that is generally ground on stone. They eat many of the roots that grow on their land or near it. The roots are pounded and ground into a flour that is cooked green or dry, then mashed or stewed into a porridge and eaten with a vegetable sauce. Sometimes, but very rarely, there is some meat in the sauce. Grains are treated and eaten in much the same way. Plantains, a fruit much like bananas but not as sweet and oily, and more starchy, are eaten, too. The roots most available to these people are yams, maniocs, taros, and sweet potatoes.

This kind of diet is hardly well balanced. In the cities, most of which border the South Atlantic, fish is a healthy supplement in the diet. But meat is almost as scarce in urban areas as it is in the rural areas. On an average, for example, the city dwellers in both Ghana and Liberia get no more than 10 pounds (4.5 kg) of meat in a year.

Poverty is the rule for the great majority of families in Gambia, Ghana, Liberia, and Sierra Leone. The average annual income in Freetown, the capital of Sierra Leone, is about ninety-five dollars. In the rural areas of Sierra Leone the annual income is less than seventy dollars. These figures match pretty well the general incomes of the other countries in the western bulge of Africa.

These kinds of incomes go a long way toward explaining the educational and health problems of the four countries. The governments of these countries have made and are making great efforts to meet these problems and do something about them. But Gambia, Ghana, Liberia, and Sierra Leone, despite their wealth in diamonds, gold, metal ores, rubber, and other agricultural products, are very poor countries. They have actually managed to accomplish much with the very little capital they have.

4
RELIGION

For centuries both Christians and Muslims have tried to convert the peoples of Africa to their faith. Except in tiny Gambia, where 85 percent of the population is Muslim, neither has been very successful.

Christian missionaries were most successful in Ghana, where 43 percent of the people are Christian. Only 10 percent of the people of Liberia and only 6 percent of the people of Sierra Leone follow the Christian faith.

Islam, the religion of the Muslims, was carried into West Africa by Muslim merchants from North Africa and Berber converts from the Sahara region. Still, Muslims account for only 12 percent of the population of Ghana, 15 percent in Liberia, and 28 percent in Sierra Leone. And even among the converts to Christianity and Islam, there are great numbers of people who are privately devoted to their old African beliefs, faiths, and practices.

The African religions are many. They have different names for their gods and many different versions of the creation of the world. Nevertheless, they have very much in common.

They all believe there is one supreme god and that this deity created the world and everything that is in it. They also believe, in common, that the supreme god is just too far away somewhere, and much too busy to be troubled by the daily affairs of the people down on earth. It is the lesser gods, spirits, ancestors, and demons who are closer to the people, who respond to the prayers of the people and to their sacrifices and other rituals.

African prayers are generally for good health, good crops, good hunting. They also make sure to declare, in their prayers, that they are innocent of any intention to do evil. Their sacrifices, generally of chickens and goats, are made to rid themselves of such evils as crop failures, any bad turn in their fortunes, and sickness. They believe, strongly, that people would live forever, happily and well, if it were not for evil forces.

Whenever an evil force strikes an African of one of the old faiths, he or she seeks out a diviner to discover the source of the misfortune. To discover this source, the diviner will throw palm nuts and read them, or toss snake bones, or read the entrails of a sacrificed chicken, or go into a trance and become possessed of some ancestor, spirit, or god.

Once the source of the evil has been disclosed, the diviner will lead a ritual in which the client gets in touch with an ancestor, a spirit, or a god, generally for the purpose of appeasement. Often, the ritual includes the sacrifice of a goat or chicken, depending on the severity of the evil the diviner has revealed. The blood of the animal is smeared on the one who is making the sacrifice, and on the emblems of the one to whom the sacrifice is made. The diviner will also provide the client with charms. If the evil has caused illness, the diviner provides medicines.

Incidentally, the sacrificed goat or chicken, once the rituals are concluded, is cooked and eaten by the entire community.

There are a variety of gods among the old African faiths, depending generally on the area in which the worshipers live. Those who depend on rain for their crops will have a rain god. Hunters will have an animal god, the god depending on the animal hunted. Those who gather palm nuts for their livelihood will have a tree god. And each ethnic group will have a different name for the same kind of god, including the faraway and greatest god.

The old African faiths have at times been called primitive and nothing more than superstition. They do not differ much, however, from the faiths of the Greeks, Romans, and Egyptians of ancient and great cultures.

5

EDUCATION

There is an eagerness for education everywhere in Africa, particularly in the western bulge. More than half the students in high school want to go on to college. Most college students say that their country's greatest need is more schools, more education. They see education as the way to a richer, healthier, and happier country, and to better government.

Nevertheless, the great majority in these countries can neither read nor write. Only some 10 percent of the people over fifteen years old in Gambia, Liberia, and Sierra Leone are literate. Ghana is somewhat better with a literacy rate of about 25 percent. Still, those who can neither read nor write are as eager to learn as those who can.

Children will often gather before a village school on a rainy morning, hoping that the teacher will let them take the places of those who couldn't come because of the weather. There just aren't enough schools to take care of all the children. And grown men and women prize the simple primers of their children and will spend hours studying them.

Even the poorest villages build their own schoolhouses with

*Two children share a book in a public
school outside of Accra, the capital of Ghana.*

material that has been given them without charge. Volunteer hands will do the constructing. And the villagers raise money to send the brighter children to schools that may be far from home, in the larger towns and cities.

There are, however, exceptions. Muslims are inclined to distrust any but their own religious teachers. Others fear that too much education might introduce foreign languages and customs and disrupt the harmony of their communities.

Girls in the rural areas suffer most for these fears. Villagers, on the whole, still believe that a girl can learn everything she needs to know at home. Marriage rather than education is the goal for women, and the earlier the marriage the better. Still, the girls and women of West Africa are attending schools of all levels and in greater numbers every year.

West Africans generally are better educated than the peoples of other parts of the African continent. There were teachers among the freed slaves who came to Sierra Leone in 1792, and they started a school immediately. By the following year there there were as many as three hundred students in their schools. Christian missionaries established schools in Gambia as early as 1826. Sierra Leone founded its Fourah College in 1827. Ghana established its Achimota College in 1924, when it was still the British colony of Gold Coast.

In 1961, in Addis Ababa, Ethiopia, a conference of African ministers of education set 1980 as the target date for six years of compulsory education for all of Africa's children. It has proved to be too ambitious a target for the new and poor African nations. They didn't have the money with which to build sufficient schools, or to provide the necessary educational equipment. Nor did they have enough teachers for the potential load of students.

Sierra Leone, for example, had room for only one of every three children in its schools. By 1975 fewer than one out of four of its children attended classes. Gambia couldn't do as well. Only 18 percent of its children were in school.

Liberia, whose schools have quadrupled in recent years, and which has increased its high school enrollment sevenfold, still has no more than 33 percent of its children in classes, and few stay on beyond the third grade. Ghana, the best of the four, has less than 45 percent of its children in school.

The situation will improve, undoubtedly, because of the Africans' respect for education. Progress, however, primarily because of the lack of funds, will be slow.

6

THE BATTLE FOR HEALTH

There is no more important problem for the West Africans than the health of its people. Sickness and death take a terrible toll on African life. A comparison of death rates with those of our own country is appalling.

In the United States the death rate, annually, is 9 of every thousand inhabitants. On an average, there are more than 21 deaths per thousand in Gambia, Ghana, Liberia, and Sierra Leone. The death rate of infants born in these countries is an average of 154 for every thousand. In the United States the death rate of infants is 14.5, and in the United Kingdom, it is 13.7.

The life expectancy in West Africa is just about 45 years, though some do live to a riper old age. In the United States life expectancy for men is 68.7 years; for women, 76.5 years.

There are several reasons for these dreadful West African figures. First, there are the diseases: pneumonia, sleeping sickness, malaria, tuberculosis, yaws, river blindness, and worm infections. Impure water accounts for many of these diseases.

Second, unbalanced diets make Africans more vulnerable to illness of all kinds and weaken their ability to fight off any

[27]

disorder. Also, there is a marked lack of proteins in the foods the African eats.

Third, there is a woeful lack of doctors in West Africa: one doctor for every 20,000 Africans. In the United States there is one doctor for every 520 people. Ghana has few more than 500 doctors, most in the urban centers. Sierra Leone has few more than one hundred doctors, all educated abroad. There are even fewer doctors in Gambia and Liberia.

The most beautiful building in any given West African city is usually its hospital, indicating the seriousness with which Africans approach the health problem, but there are not nearly enough hospitals to meet the need. Ghana has about 150 hospitals, but both Liberia and Sierra Leone have fewer than 35.

A fourth reason for poor health conditions in these West African countries is the manner in which far too many of its peoples treat their ailments.

Traditionally, the uneducated, and too often the educated, will go to a medicine man when ill. The medicine man will read the entrails of a slaughtered chicken to discover the cause of the ailment, then offer the sick person herbs, chants, and charms as a cure. Psychologically, the medicine man may help ailing people, but he is not going to cure them.

Efforts have been made to clean up the waters of West Africa. However, many polluted ponds and rivers are still used for both drinking and bathing, causing continual health problems in the area.

It has already been noted that West Africa is well aware of its health problems. The West Africans have made the building of new hospitals a priority, and new hospitals are constantly in the planning stage or being erected. Medical schools in all their universities are a priority, too. And a great deal of effort is spent in expanding the corps of nurses, technicians, and hospital technical facilities.

It is recognized in all these countries, too, that the main task in meeting health problems lies in the prevention of illness among their people. Much money and energy has been spent in this crucial direction.

Much has been done to clean up the waters in these countries, water that is rife with disease-bearing wastes, including human waste. Insecticides are being used to rid marshes, and other low-lying areas, of disease-bearing insects, such as the sleeping sickness-bearing tsetse fly. Special teams of paramedics are sent into the rural regions with disease-preventing vaccines and serums. And much is done by the different governments to educate their people in proper diet, proper health habits, and the need to see the proper person, a doctor, when they fall ill.

All these programs have been somewhat limited, unfortunately, by the resistance of the people to any change in their traditions. More seriously, they have been limited by a lack of funds.

The United Nations and the United States have provided some technical assistance, but while the aid has been welcomed and helpful, it has scarcely begun to attack the profound health problems of these peoples. At the moment West Africa needs massive aid in this area but, unhappily, is not likely to get it.

7
GOLD, DIAMONDS, COCOA

The first European traders came to the bulge of West Africa for its gold. Ghana, and Liberia as well still produce some of the precious metal, and Ghana is the fifth leading producer of gold in the world. But South Africa, Canada, the United States, and even Japan mine more gold than Ghana. South Africa produces almost forty times the gold that is found in Ghana.

There are diamonds in Ghana, too, and in Sierra Leone, and both are among the world's leaders in the mining of the gem. Sierra Leone, it is believed, has the richest deposit of alluvial diamonds (that is, found in the sediments of rivers and streams) in the world. Yet, Zaire produces about five times as many diamonds as Ghana, and seven times the diamonds Sierra Leone produces.

Still, gold and diamonds produce much of the foreign revenue the nations of the West African bulge manage to collect.

There are other precious natural resources in the bulge. There are manganese and bauxite, particularly in Ghana and Liberia. Bauxite is the source ore for the manufacture of aluminum. There are iron mines in Liberia and Sierra Leone. Liberia was the third largest exporter of iron ore in the world in 1967, and is still among the ten leading exporters of the ore.

Sierra Leone, it is believed, has the second largest deposit of the mineral rutile in the world, but it is located in areas difficult to reach. There is probably oil in the region, too, that has yet to be tapped. Only recently, in 1979, the Phillips Petroleum Company of the United States signed an agreement with the government of Ghana to start oil explorations off the Ghana coast.

Mining, however, is not the only source of revenue for the West African bulge. The region is rich with agricultural products. It is lush with fruits and nuts and vegetables and forests. Liberia, Sierra Leone, and Ghana are rich in cacao beans, from which chocolates and cocoa are made. Ghana exports one-third of the world's supply of cacao beans. Liberia exports an exceptionally good coffee. Gambia and Sierra Leone export palm kernels. Ninety-five percent of Gambia's exports are peanuts. Lumber is exported by Ghana. And Liberia is among the world's ten leaders in the production of natural rubber. It was, in fact, the chief source of natural rubber for the Allies during World War II.

In addition, Liberia has an important crop of sugarcane and tobacco. Ghana grows a considerable crop of cotton, as well as coffee and tobacco. And there is lumber everywhere in the region.

Eighty-five percent of the people of Gambia, more than half the people of Ghana, seventy-five percent of the people of Liberia, and more than three-quarters of the people of Sierra Leone are involved with the agricultural production of their countries. Except for the few larger agricultural industries, such as natural rubber and lumber, most farms are small. The average farm consists of no more than 4 or 5 acres (1.6 or 2.0 hectares). A recent development in farming has been the creation of cooperatives. Cooperatives, where people can pool their money, tools, and resources, are better able to purchase the modern farming tools and equipment that are very much lacking in this area.

Fish are plentiful in the waters off the coasts of the bulge of West Africa, but most of the people of the region live inland and fishing is not one of their foremost industries. There is also a rather insignificant herding of cattle and sheep. Meat is not a staple of the diet of West Africa and it is believed that snails provide the West Africans with most of the protein in their diet.

Manufacturing in the bulge is just beginning to develop. Ghana, for example, is just beginning to manufacture steel, tires, and smelters to turn bauxite into aluminum. It is also beginning to refine oil. Liberia is beginning to develop the facilities to manufacture soap, plastics, paint, paper products, textiles, and fertilizer. But there is a great lack of machinery of all kinds in West Africa, and very little money with which to purchase these machines.

The bulge, however, does not lack for artisans and craftspeople. In the city stores and in the marketplaces there is abundant evidence of their dexterity. Africa has been known for its arts and crafts, particularly for its magnificent work in ivory, wood, and stone. Much of this work may be seen in museums around the world.

The Gambian artisans and craftspeople turn out beautiful leatherwork and hand-designed cotton batik fabrics. Their exquisitely hand-wrought gold and silver jewelry, and particularly their filigree work, have been influenced by their Muslim cultures.

In Ghana the artisans and craftspeople produce, in addition to gold and silver jewelry and objects, magnificent wood carvings, pottery, and wickerwork. They also continue to make all the traditional paraphernalia worn or carried by the old chieftains.

Sierra Leone's artisans and craftspeople continue the tradition of making wooden face masks, as well as ritual figures and staffs. They are also most adept with pottery, basket weaving, and hand-painted cloths. Liberia, too, has its share of artisans and craftspeople producing similar work for its shops and markets.

There is one other occupation that flourishes, on a small but important scale, in Sierra Leone and Liberia: smuggling, particularly of diamonds.

There is a tax in Sierra Leone for diamond diggers, and there is a good deal of illegal digging for diamonds as a result. There is also a tax on the exportation of diamonds, and this has led to considerable smuggling of diamonds out of Sierra Leone and across the border into Liberia. It is believed that the diamonds smuggled out of Sierra Leone far outweigh the diamonds legally exported from the country.

The efforts of both the government and mining companies to stop this contraband have so far proved ineffective. Monrovia, the capital city of Liberia, offers diamonds at cut-rate prices. In fact, diamond trading is one of Liberia's best-organized businesses.

8

GAMBIA

Gambia is one of the smallest of all countries, smaller than the state of Connecticut, with a population of less than 585,000, one-sixth the population of Connecticut.

At its widest point it is no wider than 30 miles (48 km). It stretches along both banks of the Gambia River for some 200 miles (322 km) with U-shaped Senegal on both its sides. The Gambians speak of their own country as a finger resting in the jaws of Senegal.

Most of its people are poor nomads or farmers growing just about enough food to keep their families alive. A good many, however, do better for themselves by illegal means, smuggling goods across their borders.

In recent years farm advisors from Taiwan have come to teach the Gambians how to develop their rice crops. This has been a great help, since rice is Gambia's main food staple.

The development of the tourist industry has been helpful, too. The ride up the Gambia River has been its main attraction. The trip affords an excellent view of tropical trees, flowers, and colorful birds. For Americans and others interested in

*An impromptu dance celebration in
Juffure, Gambia. Juffure is the village
made famous in Alex Haley's book,* Roots.

genealogy, there is Juffure, the small village that was the birthplace of Alex Haley's ancestors. Haley is the American author who amazingly traced his ancestors back to their origins, and recorded his findings in a book called *Roots*.

Another curiosity in Gambia is the field of thirty-four concentric, stone circles near McCarthy Island, structures that range from a few inches to some 10 feet (3 m) in height. The stones are very much like those erected by Druids, an ancient religious people of Great Britain. Some say that they were erected by Carthaginians who sailed up the Gambia River many years before Christ was born.

Banjul, the capital of Gambia, with its population of about 51,700, is itself something of a curiosity. It was known as Bathurst when it was a British territory and it remains very British in character. The people dress after the style of Britain. They go to tea in the afternoon, and their favorite sport is cricket. Their streets are named after the generals of the Duke of Wellington, who defeated Napoleon at Waterloo, and their buses are double-deckers, like those in London.

But Banjul does not look like London at all. It has very few modern buildings and most of its people live in tin huts. There are no public movies or dance halls. Tourists, however, are entertained by a variety of shows the hotels offer, among them the drum-beating ritual dances, accompanied by the kora, balafong, and balanbota, instruments native to Gambia.

HISTORY

During the eighteenth and nineteenth centuries, Gambia was a battleground in the wars between the Muslims and, mainly, the Marabout and Soninki peoples of the country. The British brought an end to the conflicts by promising protection to each side.

From 1821 to 1843 Gambia was governed by a British governor-general posted in Sierra Leone. In 1843 Gambia became a British Crown Colony, a colony belonging to the king of England, and Bathurst (Banjul) became the seat of government and the capital of the country.

In 1965 Gambia became an independent country. In 1970 it became a republic but remained part of the British Commonwealth of Nations, along with Canada, Australia, and a number of other countries around the world. Sir Dawda K. Jawara was elected its first president, for a five-year term, in 1972.

Gambia's parliament consists of thirty-seven voting members, and includes four chiefs of four different ethnic groups, and an attorney general.

Under Jawara, who was reelected to the presidency in 1977, Gambia has seen some improvement in its agriculture and in its tourist trade. It remains a very poor country but it has avoided the hazards of the swift industrialization experienced by other Third World countries, particularly the mounting of huge debts and the tremendous interest payments such debts involve.

9
GHANA

Ghana is about the size of Illinois and Indiana combined, 92,000 square miles (238,000 sq km). It has a population of about eight and a half million, more than half of which lives in its capital city, Accra. About a quarter of a million live in its second largest city, Kumasi. Kumasi was the capital of the ancient Ashanti Empire and is one of the oldest cities in West Africa. Another 161,000 people live in the Sekondi-Takoradi area, around the growing seaport of Takoradi.

More than half the people of Ghana are employed in agriculture, but there has been great effort to industrialize the country. The effort has met with some success. However, it has created a number of problems.

First, there has been considerable resistance to industrialization by a people who are accustomed to living in small communities and maintaining the traditions and customs of their ancestors. Second, Ghana, once one of the richest countries in Africa, borrowed great sums of money to finance these projects, and is now deeply in debt. Huge national debts make for inflation, and the rate of inflation in Ghana has met with much protest, and even rebellion.

Among other efforts to build up its revenues, Ghana, like Gambia, is trying to build its tourist trade. Its main attraction is its great number of forts and castles along its 350-mile (560-km) coastline.

The forts were built by the Portuguese, Danes, Germans, and British as early as the seventeenth century. The structures were constantly attacked by one or another of the European invaders, and sometimes captured, sometimes destroyed. When they were destroyed, new forts and castles were erected in their places.

There are twenty-four such old forts and castles, in various states of repair. All that remains of some of them is ruins. Most of these old structures have been declared national monuments by the government of Ghana and much money has been spent to restore and to keep these historical buildings intact. The Cape Coast Castle, for example, on Cape Coast, was the site of the British headquarters from 1665 to 1876. Today it houses the West African Historical Museum.

HISTORY

Before the arrival of the European traders, Ghana was a land of a number of independent kingdoms and chiefdoms which, centuries before, had been under the influence of the great African empires. The Portuguese were the first to establish a settlement in Ghana. The Dutch and Germans and English followed.

When Britain declared slave trading illegal in 1807, the Portuguese, Dutch, and Germans withdrew from the country.

The British remained and in 1874 declared Gold Coast, as Ghana was called in those days, a British colony.

A region known as the Northern Territories was annexed to Gold Coast in 1901. The inland Ashanti kingdom, after seventy-five years of fierce resistance, was finally forced to yield to the British invaders and was annexed to Gold Coast, too, in 1901. Part of Togoland, which had been a German colony, was added to Gold Coast, after the defeat of Germany in World War I.

Following World War II, the world experienced a great surge of nationalism. People in all parts of the globe, and particularly those in Africa, demanded and fought for the right to be governed by their own people. This was the beginning of the end of European colonialism and the beginning of independence for the African nations.

The British, many of whom were not opposed to independence for their colonies, introduced a number of changes in the governmental administration of Gold Coast. These were not sufficient, however, to please the people of Gold Coast who wanted complete freedom from foreign domination.

One of the greatest and most controversial leaders in Africa's battle for independence was Kwame Nkrumah. Nkrumah was born in a small village in Ghana. He left his country for the United States, where he lived for ten years. In the United States he studied at Lincoln University and at the University of Pennsylvania, working at any kind of job he could get. At different times he was a dishwasher, a waiter, a fish peddler, and he worked in a soap factory as well. During this period of his life, there were times when he was so poor he had to sleep in the subways because he had no place else to go.

After his ten years in the United States, Nkrumah left for England, where he studied at the highly prestigious London School of Economics. It was while he was in London that he became involved in Ghana's drive for independence from Britain. He was an exceptionally good organizer and quickly became a leader in the movement. He was jailed by the British for his rebel activities, and it was actually while he was in a British prison that he was elected to head the preindependent government of Gold Coast. The preindependent government had been established by the English in an effort to maintain its hold in the country and to hold off the complete independence the people were demanding.

The British tactics, however, could not halt the nationalist movement in Gold Coast. In 1957, while remaining within the British Commonwealth of Nations, Gold Coast became Ghana, an independent country. Nkrumah was elected its first president.

There are differences of opinion about the way Nkrumah conducted his office. There is no doubt that he worked hard to unite the peoples of Ghana, to build schools and hospitals as well as the economy of the country. Today more than 50 percent of the people of Ghana are literate and thousands of its educated people are experienced in government administration, business, and all the professions. Nkrumah is largely responsible for this. He is also largely responsible for the development of the Takoradi seaport, and for the construction of a large hydroelectric project on the Volta River, which provides much of the electricity for Ghana's developing industries.

But he did incur a huge national debt which has made for Ghana's high rate of inflation. Worse, in the eyes of most people, he established a one-party rule in Ghana, and a virtual dictatorship.

Nevertheless, he was idolized by his people who called him Never Failing or Ever Giving Leader or the Giant of Ghana.

However, Nkrumah lost the support of the city people because, among other reasons, he trampled on civil rights, arresting and imprisoning a countless number of his opponents. He lost support in the rural communities because, in his efforts to unite all the peoples of Ghana, he cut down the power of the inland chiefs, and because prices dropped on the cocoa market. He lost support in both urban and rural parts of the country because of Ghana's high rate of inflation.

Nevertheless, Nkrumah was reelected president in 1965. However, while he was on a visit to China in 1966, a military coup by a National Liberation Council, headed by Lieutenant General Joseph A. Ankrah, ousted Nkrumah from office.

Ankrah suspended the constitution of Ghana and ruled the country until 1969. In 1969 Ankrah admitted he had received money from private companies for political purposes, and was forced to resign.

His place was taken by another military man, Brigadier General Akwasi Afrifa. Under Afrifa, in August 1969, Ghana once again enjoyed the privilege of free national elections and elected Kofi Busia, a civilian, the second president of the Republic of Ghana. Busia was the leader of the party that had opposed Nkrumah. It was Busia's party that won the majority of seats in Ghana's National Assembly (congress or parliament).

Busia enjoyed his presidency, however, for less than two and a half years, before another military coup once more destroyed the young republic. This time, and again while the president of the country was abroad, it was Colonel Ignatius Kutu Acheampong who was the leader of the coup. Again, the constitution of Ghana was scrapped and a military dictatorship installed.

The dictatorship lasted for seven and a half years, until 1979. It was upset at that time by still another military man, Flight Lieutenant J. J. Rawlings, chairman of the Armed Forces Revolutionary Council.

But Rawlings had no dictatorial ambitions. He declared the council favored a return to a democratic form of government. Ghana became for the third time a republic, and Dr. Hilla Limann was elected its first president.

10
LIBERIA

Liberia, with an area of 43,000 square miles (111,000 sq km), is about the size of Ohio. Its population of less than two million is a little smaller than the population of Cleveland, Ohio. Its largest and most important city is Monrovia, with a population of about 229,000. Like the other countries in the West African bulge, the vast majority of its peoples live in the farmlands and woodlands. Nearly half of Liberia is covered by dense jungles.

There are two distinct groups of people in Liberia, the peoples who are the descendants of its original inhabitants and those who are the descendants of the freed American slaves who settled in the country in 1822. The descendants of the American freedmen constitute little more than 1 percent of the population of Liberia, but until April 1980, they were completely in control of its business, its commerce, and its government.

Most of the descendants of American freedmen live in Monrovia, the capital of the country, named after the American president, James Monroe. America is, for them, the motherland, much as England is the motherland for Australians, New Zealanders, and some Canadians. They name their towns after cities and towns and states in the United States, like Buchanan and Maryland. They dress in the manner of Americans or as they imagine Americans dress. For formal affairs they wear formal jackets and top hats. The houses of the more wealthy are patterned after the mansions of the old southern estates and plantations. They established themselves as the elite of the country. "Elite" is even the term they used to name themselves.

In fact, in Monrovia there were distinct names for the different peoples living in the capital. The Elite Society consisted of some twenty families of America-Liberian descent, plus a few families of tribal origin. The Honorables, more than half of whom were America-Liberians, held a number of important government positions. They were also the doctors, lawyers, and clergymen. Those who were called Civilized, about one-third America-Liberians and two-thirds of tribal origin, were the minor officials, schoolteachers, nurses, and some of the skilled craftspeople.

Indeterminate was the name given students and people not sure what category they belonged to. The Indeterminates were all of tribal origin. So were those Monrovia called Tribal. They were the laborers, stevedores, fishermen, small traders, and even some wealthy traders who maintained the tribal life-style.

The Tribal, the Indeterminate, and even some of the Civilized were treated as second-class citizens, while the Elite pocketed the revenues of the country for their own private purposes.

The Elite had been accused of limiting, or ignoring, the education of the bulk of Liberia's population, of which 75 percent can neither read nor write. They had been accused of al-

Affluence and poverty are neighbors in Monrovia, Liberia, where high-rise buildings and houses overlook tin shacks on the beach.

most completely disregarding the miserable poverty of the great majority of Liberia's people, as well as ignoring the dreadfully unhealthy conditions in which they lived. They were even accused, in the early 1930s, of practicing slavery.

On April 12, 1980, a bloody coup, led by Master Sergeant Samuel K. Doe, brought about an abrupt change in the affairs of that country. President William R. Tolbert was killed. A number of the Elite were executed. Sergeant Doe, announcing that the purpose of the coup was to end corruption and ineffective government, became the head of state. He established a cabinet of fifteen to help him run the country. Five members of the cabinet were army officers. At least four of its members belonged to the People's Progress Party, and had been jailed by the Tolbert government and released immediately after the coup. The People's Progressive Party had been banned by Tolbert, after the party had called for a general strike to unseat the Tolbert regime.

The Elite no longer control the government or the people of Liberia. The future of the country, however, remains uncertain.

HISTORY

In 1816, a group of American abolitionists organized the American Colonization Society. Its purpose was to find and create a homeland for freed American slaves who wanted to return to Africa. Six years later, the first of these freedmen landed on Providence Island in Liberia. The island was bought, at gunpoint, from a local chieftain for $300 worth of trading goods. The black Americans named their colony Monrovia. From the beginnings the Afro-Americans intended to keep their ties with the United States, calling themselves Americo-Liberians.

The colony survived both the unhealthy conditions that were encountered and the numerous attacks by local chiefs. With more trading goods, the colony bought additional land from friendlier or greedier chieftains. The territory they occupied sizeable now, the Americo-Liberians named the territory, their new country, Liberia, after the Latin word *liber,* meaning "free."

Until 1847 the Africans called their new home the Liberian Commonwealth. In that year the Commonwealth's governor, Joseph Jenkins Roberts, a Virginia-born freeman, declared Liberia a republic. It was the first black republic in Africa. Joseph Jenkins Roberts was its first president. Its constitution and Congress were patterned after those of the United States.

Before the military coup of 1980, Liberia's political history was free of dramatic events. It experienced no coups, no uprisings, no rebellions. From 1877 until 1980, the reins of government were in the hands of the True Whig party. The Whig party in the United States became the Republican party, the party of Abraham Lincoln. In Liberia the True Whig party was the only recognized political party until 1980.

William V. S. Tubman, a True Whig, was president of Liberia from 1943 until his death in 1971. William R. Tolbert, Jr., succeeded to the presidency on the death of Tubman and was president of Liberia until the Samuel Doe coup in 1980.

The economic history of Liberia has been comparatively less stable, however. For some years Liberia exported the finest coffee in the world; their cane sugar and *ca,* wood from which dyes are produced, brought a great deal of revenue into the country's treasury.

But the Germans invented synthetic dyes. Beet sugar put an end to much of the profits in sugarcane. Brazil took the coffee

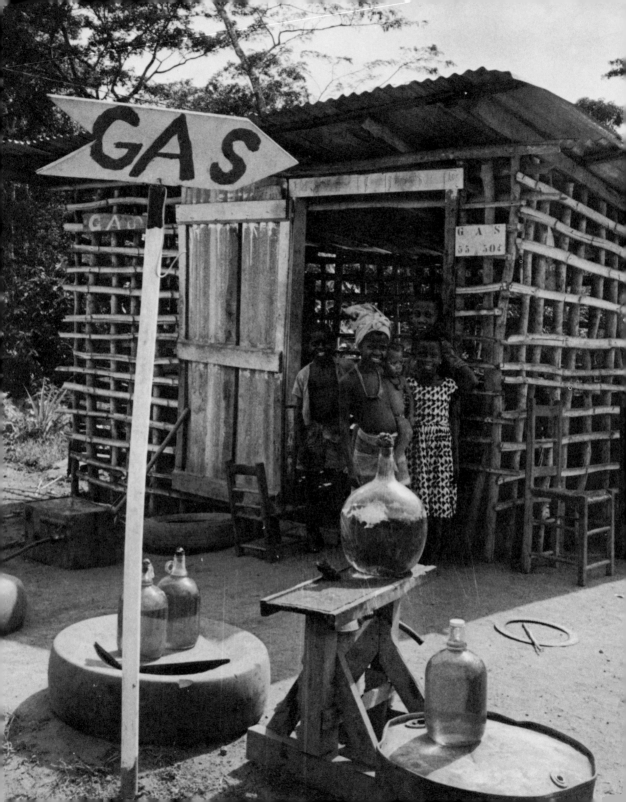

trade away from Liberia. And the European countries preferred to buy from their own colonies, while the United States began to trade with South America for its tropical products.

Times were bad economically in Liberia until foreign investment came in to save the country from bankruptcy.

In 1923 the Firestone Tire and Rubber Company moved into Liberia. They leased almost a million acres (400,000 hectares) of rubber country for a period of ninety-nine years. By 1950, 90 percent of Liberia's exports were rubber. The economy picked up. The big Robertsfield airport was built. A new seaport was developed in Monrovia. Liberia built its first modern highways, principally for the moving of rubber to its ports.

In 1955 huge iron deposits were discovered in Liberia's Mount Nimba. More capital, mainly Swedish and American, flowed into the country. Iron ore became the fastest-growing export for Liberia.

Liberia has one other source of considerable income. Ship registration is inexpensive in Liberia. Its inspection of the seaworthiness of ships is not particularly rigid. As a consequence, shipping companies from all over the globe register their ships and tankers in Monrovia, and sail under the Liberian flag. Fifty-three percent of the enormous fleet of "Liberian" ships are owned by Greek shipowners. Forty-three percent belong to

A sign points the way to the
gas pumps at a roadside
gas station in Liberia.

American companies. Liberia, which in 1960 did not have one merchant ship, and which has few such ships today, collects about one million dollars every year for its services and accommodations to fleet owners the world around.

For all these revenues, however, Liberia is shouldered with enormous debts. It is still a poor country. Whether Samuel K. Doe and his Army Redemption Council can turn Liberia's economy around and bring prosperity to Liberia and its people is still to be seen.

11

SIERRA LEONE

About the size of South Carolina, Sierra Leone has an area of about 28,000 square miles (73,000 sq km). It has a population of about three million, of which 90 percent live in the rural areas of the country. Seventy percent of its urban people live in Freetown, Sierra Leone's one large city, and its capital. A small minority of its people are the descendants of freed slaves from Britain, Canada, and Nova Scotia, as well as of a number of slaves who fled to freedom from the West Indies. Most of them live in Freetown or in the small villages around it. They are known as Creoles, or Krios, in Sierra Leone. The vast majority are descendants of the area's original inhabitants, and those who moved into the country from other regions in Africa.

Seventy-five percent of the people of Sierra Leone depend on the farming of their small landholdings for a living. Twenty-three percent are miners of diamonds, iron ore, bauxite, and rutile. Only 6 percent of the population work in manufacturing shops. The rest are involved in some kind of service work.

Many of the first Creoles to arrive in Sierra Leone were doctors, lawyers, teachers, scientists, writers, and clergymen. They were proud to call themselves "black Englishmen." Their descendants are still the most educated people in the country, the most affluent, and the most politically powerful.

An oddity among the people of Sierra Leone is its number of secret societies, each with its own special features. The Wunde Society, for example, teaches its members bravery and endurance of pain. The Gola and Porro societies go in for acrobatic dances, and other dances that require physical strength. The Sande Society is limited to women singers and dancers.

Another oddity in Sierra Leone is the soapstone figurine that is occasionally found in its riverbeds. These figurines, miniature sculptures of men, were apparently carved many, many years ago by some earlier people of Sierra Leone. The ancestors of the people native to Sierra Leone were skilled craftsmen. Their ivory carvings were especially magnificent.

It is believed that these figurines were supposed to be the embodiment of the spirits of perhaps important tribal leaders who had died. Today, when anyone finds such a sculpture in a riverbed, he or she treasures it. The figurine, it is believed in Sierra Leone, ensures a good rice crop. Rice, as in other West African countries, is the main staple of the diet of Sierra Leone's people.

HISTORY

Originally, as in the rest of West Africa, Sierra Leone was divided into a number of small, independent kingdoms and chiefdoms.

In 1460 Pedro da Cintra, a Portuguese explorer, visited the area and called it Serra Lyoa (Lion Mountain). Serra Lyoa became known as Sierra Leone.

During the seventeenth and eighteenth centuries Sierra

Leone was a haunt for pirates. In 1787 a ship carrying freedmen from the British Isles landed in Sierra Leone. As American abolitionists were to do shortly afterward, the British abolitionists had secured a home for Britain's ex-slaves. Sierra Leone became the first home in Africa for freedmen.

The British ex-slaves called their first settlement in Sierra Leone Province of Freedom. The constitution they wrote for the government of the province was even more democratic than the English constitution at the end of the eighteenth century. There was great hope in the settlement. But they were attacked by the native Temne people, from whom they had taken the land, and the settlement was destroyed.

In 1792 the British made a second attempt to create a home for ex-slaves. A number of freedmen had fought for the British and against the Americans in the war of American Independence. At the end of the war, with the Americans the victors, the ex-slaves escaped to Nova Scotia. It was a thousand of these freedmen living in Nova Scotia who settled, successfully, in Sierra Leone, in a colony they named Freetown.

Eight years later the colony was strengthened by the arrival of 550 Maroons, slaves who had escaped to freedom in the West Indies. Another 2,000 freedmen joined the colony later.

When British ships, after Britain had outlawed slave trading, intercepted slave ships, the slaves they freed were landed in Freetown. By 1834 the population in Freetown had swelled to thirty-two thousand.

In the interim, in 1808 Britain had proclaimed the settlement a Crown Colony. Almost ninety years later, in 1896, Britain declared the interior regions of Sierra Leone a protectorate, but not before putting down a number of rebellions

*This scene of children drawing water from a
community water pipe, is typical of the poverty
that continues to exist in Sierra Leone.*

by the Temne and Mende people who refused to pay taxes imposed on them by the British.

Independence came slowly to Sierra Leone. It wasn't until 1924 that Britain allowed chiefs in the protectorate to run for seats in the country's national council. It wasn't until 1943, during World War II, that Africans were permitted in the executive council of the government. It wasn't until 1951 that Britain was required, because of the rising tide of nationalism, to give the country a constitution that laid down the framework for eventual independence.

Ten years later, in 1961, Sierra Leone, at last, became an independent country, with Sir Milton Margai as its first prime minister.

Sir Milton Margai was a man of exceptional learning. He had earned his degree in medicine at the University of Edinburgh. Under his leadership Sierra Leone was politically stable and prospered. But Sir Milton Margai died in 1964. His brother, Sir Albert Margai, became prime minister. At this point things went from bad to worse. Sir Albert Margai was accused of corruption and was forced to resign in 1967.

In 1967 Siaka Stevens was elected prime minister but was ousted from office by an army coup, only minutes after he had been sworn in.

A year later a second army coup reinstated Stevens. A third military coup failed, as did two attempts to assassinate the prime minister. In 1971 Stevens declared Sierra Leone a republic, with himself as president.

In 1973 Stevens ran for reelection. The police, which he controlled, prevented the campaigning of any opposition. The opposition boycotted the elections. Siaka Stevens was elected overwhelmingly. Sierra Leone, unhappily, is a one-party country.

FOR FURTHER READING

Bohannan, P. *Africa and Africans*. New York: Natural History Press, 1964.

Fage, J. D. *A History of Africa*. New York: Knopf, 1978.

Hallett, R. *Africa Since 1875*. Ann Arbor, Michigan: University of Michigan Press, 1974.

July, R. W. *A History of the African People*. New York: Scribners, 1974.

Kane, R. S. *Africa A to Z*. Garden City, New York: Doubleday, 1972.

Murphy, J. E. *Understanding Africa*. New York: T. Y. Crowell, 1978.

INDEX